Best of luck,
Bill Frank

W9-BTB-243

the
advertising
on-ramp

The Advertising On-Ramp

getting your **first**
advertising **job**

BELLE FRANK

Executive Vice President
Director of Strategy & Research
Young & Rubicam
New York, New York

Paramount Market Publishing, Inc.

Paramount Market Publishing, Inc.
950 Danby Road, Suite 136
Ithaca, NY 14850
www.paramountbooks.com
Voice: 607-275-8100; 888-787-8100   Fax: 607-275-8101

Publisher: James Madden
Editorial Director: Doris Walsh

Copyright © 2013 Young & Rubicam, Inc.
First published USA 2013
Printed in USA

Cataloging in Publication Data available
ISBN-10: 0-9851795-1-1
ISBN-13: 978-0-9851795-1-9

Contents

Hiring and developing great talent means getting past the resume.

Preface

Never before has the advertising C-suite talked more about our commitment to hiring and developing great talent. And yet never before has it been so hard for young people to break into our business. **This disconnect between what Mad Ave employers need and what Mad Ave "rushees" want often comes down to miscommunication.** With the best of intentions, young, promising candidates say the wrong things. What gets lost in translation is the unique differentiation the best candidates bring and the best way to clue employers in to what great talent they are. Newbies need to do a better job on their scripts so employers get past their resumes and see who they can become.

Y&R has published this book because we want to help the best young people come to Y&R so that we can be sure we can give our clients the talent they need when they work with us. The more we **help great young people find their way in**, the better we will drive client business (and our own!) now and into the future.

—BELLE FRANK
JANUARY 2013

Fostering the best environment for sustained success.

Why this book?

Y&R Global CEO **David Sable** on how this book came to be

We all want to work for a great company. A company with a strong culture. A place where we feel we belong and can make a difference. In turn, companies, and especially leaders of companies, like to believe that they **foster the best environment for success**. Perhaps the ultimate test of a great company is one that endures, that thrives over time. Young & Rubicam is one of those rare success stories—a company that remains relevant because of its capacity to reinvent itself for every generation.

My first job in the industry was at Y&R in 1976. Y&R had the most **incredible training program, truly the gold standard of the industry.** It educated and equipped me in ways that still hold true today and continues to serve me and the agency well. Indeed, when I became CEO at Y&R two years ago, I knew it was critical that we focus on our culture and talent.

Y&R has a **strong values system** ingrained in the DNA of **the place.** We are committed to a vision, mission and values that help us know how to think about marketing communications today. This drives a nearly relentless focus on being an indispensable partner to our clients. Fundamental to that is **making sure we have the right people**—people who are passionate about what we do, who are continually fueled by their curiosity, their creativity and, above all, by a love of our clients.

As we state in our vision, mission and values:

People are our most important asset. In fact, they're our **only asset.** Ideas, passion, innovation and insight come from people.

What's remarkable about Y&R is the exceptional level of **loyalty** people have toward the agency—we have a group of people who have committed heart and soul over many years to the company. A group of people who **inspire and support** each other, who preserve what's best about our culture while remaining **committed to innovation**, who have been raised to **believe in collaboration** and in always **bringing the best people** to the table. Not only do we have a few 40-year tenured employees who survived industry changes and several management upheavals, we also have people who joined in the 1990s and early 2000s and stuck with us through tougher times in the industry. We have always had **many people who leave but love to come back.** There's something about our culture . . .

This combination of **strong values, embraced by earnest, committed people who care passionately about their colleagues, their clients and the work** we do has allowed Y&R to achieve continuously over many decades. And it has allowed those who have lived it personally to see first-hand the kind of people we need to succeed. It's within this culture that we find **Belle Frank,** and this book.

No one I know epitomizes the Y&R person more than Belle Frank.

I have worked with Belle for more than 20 years. We have worked on business together in several categories and I have watched her grow into a trusted advisor to her clients. When Belle collaborates with a team her energy is infectious. When she lays out strategy, her arms waving, she easily switches back and forth between complex concepts, an important issue, and the latest popular culture idea. Throughout meetings Belle never stops thinking. When you are with her you can see her mind moving at high speed, continuously questioning and exploring every opportunity from many different angles.

Belle has **all that can be expected of a top-grade professional**—a true model for how Y&R thinks about great talent. She is smart and driven. But what really makes her special, and so part of the fabric of our Y&R culture and values, is her passion for people—our clients, her colleagues, of course, but she has a special place in her heart for people just starting out in the business.

One day Belle approached me and asked for half an hour in my office. She said she had something important she wanted to talk to me about. This type of request is often made when someone is resigning or needing a change, so I approached our meeting with some trepidation. Belle had a very different sort of request. **She wanted to write a book to help young people trying to break into the advertising business by giving them a clear road map for how to do it.**

She believed the future talent of our business was being short-changed—that many **new graduates were unprepared and unsupported in their quest to enter our industry** and that we had a responsibility to do something about it.

And so we support Belle in the publication of her book. A book that takes the insight of **one of Y&R's most talented and longest-serving employees** and packages it in a way that provides **guidance for those just starting out in their careers.** It's no surprise that a book that comes from Belle's soul, also reflects the soul of Y&R. Belle grew up here and it was here she honed her professional abilities—her strategic skills, her collaborative skills and her mentoring skills. While this book grew out of Belle, it is intertwined with the vision of Y&R.

We are all about being our clients' most important partner and we can't do it if we don't have the right people. Our job is to resist the usual and develop recommendations and implementation plans for how clients and their brands should behave and communicate. **We don't manufacture products, we inspire and express new ideas.** And we can't be creative if we don't have an approach to attracting the best, most diverse talent, because **new ideas don't come from doing things the same way over and over again.** They come from **new thinking** to solve intractable problems. They come from combining existing thinking in **new ways**. They come from advances in one space that can be **repurposed** into another. People must create these ideas and so **people are the heart and soul of our business.** If we are to continue to sustain our business over time we must have the right people.

What you learn from this book is designed to help you get into our industry, which, in turn, will help *us* be better at what we do. **This book is designed to help people who are making their way out of college and into the advertising business.** It will probably be most interesting to you if you have come out of school with rich liberal arts, humanities, and social science training, but we're pretty sure a few business majors will find it helpful as well. We're not suggesting this can't help you at all if you want to go into finance or become a doctor; it's just not written for you. What we know for sure is that in our business, we see many young **beginners who are looking for the kind of help this book is designed to give.**

Belle and the rest of us at Y&R know that many talented people who are looking for the *Advertising On-Ramp* may not know exactly how to find it; with this book we are trying to reach out to them. We need a diverse employee base to ensure we've got people who can deliver for our clients. Our summer internship program and the way we approach hiring leverages our strategic understanding of how people behave so that we don't miss the hidden gems not yet polished. **This book is designed to help you showcase yourself if you are looking for the on-ramp and also includes a** section describing some of the ways we work to find the right talent for Y&R. At Y&R we believe in the lessons in this book and if you want to work in this industry, you should, too. I am confident that if you read this book, if you leverage Belle's intelligence, take the advice of one of the most conscientious people I've ever met, you will find something in its pages that will help you along your road.

A clear
road map
for young
people
trying to
break into
advertising.

The On-Ramp Situation Analysis

I'm a consumer insights expert. For 30 years I have worked to help clients understand the reality of the people who use their brands. I try to make sense of research on target audiences by synthesizing that research into actionable marketing strategies. I guess you could say I am good at using data to tell true stories about people. But I didn't look for this job. I didn't even know there was such a job when I first started working. Nevertheless I am in it and am good at it. I've been doing it for more years than most of the people starting out in the business have even been alive. And along the way I have learned **a few things that might help you** as you think about looking for your jobs.

I am fortunate to work in a company led since February 2011 by Global CEO David Sable. Y&R has long been in David's blood. He joined the Y&R training program in 1976, and he credits this induction into the business as the foundation for much of what he has done in his life. I started in the same training program in 1978. Of course, it was a very different time from now, and yet the idea that our business needed high-quality talent was evident from the focus we placed even then on hiring the best candidates.

The Advertising On-Ramp: Getting your first advertising job is designed to be **an easy-to-read book of workplace advice for college graduates** and others who are newly entering the work world of marketing communications. Young professionals who appreciate the advice can be expected to find opportunities more easily AND do better in their first career engagements. My personal experience is with the hiring of those on the business side of our industry—account management and strategy or planning—but the advice is also valuable for those searching for the creative on-ramp. While the creative department on-ramp also requires the preparation of a portfolio, those who make hiring decisions on creative talent have told me that beyond a candidate's portfolio the lessons of this book are critical for them as well.

This book speaks to **Y&R's commitment** to addressing a critical need in our industry—**attracting and retaining the best talent.** Our inability to do so limits our ability to thrive. A business of ideas like ours is only as creative as our talent. Unless we find a way of leveraging the power of an increasingly diverse workforce, we will be at a loss.

This book is important for those starting out in advertising today as well as for management in the companies that hire them. The group of young people entering the marketing world today will experience a very different business from those of earlier cohorts, including their parents. A number of important trends and values shifts have created a "perfect storm" out of which the need for this book emerged.

The problem this book wants to solve

Never has the need for great advertising talent been greater nor gotten more attention. Never has it been more difficult to break into the advertising business.

- The marketing communications industry has become more complicated and more global, and yet **we have had difficulty attracting, training, and retaining the best, most diverse talent.** This has limited the ability of many communications agencies to get the highest-quality applicants. Sometimes we lose entry-level candidates to clients or management consulting firms, which can add to the pressure we experience finding the right people to partner with our clients.

- Business problems require collaborative solutions so marketing firms need people with new kinds of what may be called "softer" leadership skills. **Employees need to be especially talented at collaboration, group project participation,** and **management.**

- While academic opportunities have opened up for diversity candidates in marketing communications, the industry has been criticized by some for failing to be as

How to find opportunities more easily and do better in your first career engagements.

inclusive as it should be. On the candidates' side, it may be that the lack of personal connections with advertising firms or personal access to marketing professionals limits their ability to break into the business. Moving forward, **it is especially critical that our business finds a way to ensure that our workforce is as diverse as our world.**

Where did this book come from?

Several years ago I attended a luncheon hosted by a professional advertising organization honoring a dear colleague's career in the business.

I had known the honoree for many years. At one time she was the director of the department in which I worked. She achieved a great deal, rising to the rank of Vice Chairman before retiring. At the time she was recognized, we had worked together for 20 years, at least 10 in close collaboration. I had come to admire her personally as well as professionally and am lucky to be able to describe her as one of my mentors. While we never used that phrase to describe our working relationship, as she was senior to me her entire career and was always **a source of advice and guidance** even when I wasn't working for her directly, I can never think of her as anything but a mentor. Since her retirement I can't really say we remain in *close* contact but I would do anything I could for her and believe that I owe her a tremendous amount in terms of anything I may have achieved in my career.

In addition to what I may think I owe her professionally or personally, I know that I owe her the foundation of this book. When my colleague rose to accept her award she spoke about her own career as having been about finding her professional **"path and voice."** And as I sat and listened to her talk, I knew that for the rest of my career I would never think about the challenges faced when advancing at work as anything but those related to "path and voice."

This book offers themes that are helpful to beginning advertising professionals. It grew out of my personal passion to make a difference and from insights I gathered about some of the barriers our industry faces to achieving our diversity goals. Using **Y&R's proprietary consumer technique eXploring,** I shared many experiences with students and professionals, those looking for work as well as those in the position to hire.

Sandy Thompson, our Global Chief Insights Officer and my current boss, brought eXploring to Y&R. eXploring is the way **we ensure our insights are based on real consumer truths.** We believe that if you want to understand how the lion hunts, you don't go to the zoo, you need to go to the veld (well the Serengeti if we are being totally accurate and less pithy)! You get the point.

When an advertising strategist like me wants to learn about the people I want to influence, I need to get out from behind my desk and share real world experiences with them or I will be drawing conclusions based on somewhat artificial circumstances. And when I share our learning to inspire our creative teams, I do it by **telling real stories about the real people I have met.** As such, I ensure our marketing is relevant because it reflects the truth of what people do. The examples presented here are based on real candidates and their journeys.

The perspective of this book was shaped a great deal by my experience teaching professional development workshops at City University of New York, an urban university whose student population draws from the ethnic diversity of the more than 8.2 million people of New York City. I learned that many highly motivated, capable candidates don't understand how to best prepare and market themselves to thrive in our business. I also learned that **managers in our business may not understand how unfamiliar these potential employees are with the demands of our industry** and that if we aren't careful we may miss some diamonds in the rough.

This book also grew out of my experience as a member of the Board of Directors of the Communications & Media Studies program at Tufts University and with my children's friends and my friends' children. One day I noticed that the workforce I managed looked, behaved and thought like my own children. Will Frank, a certified geek, has found his way to intellectual property law, but his experience also mirrored the journeys described in this book. Rebecca Frank, just past the quarter-century mark, is a social media strategist and digital analytics person for a public relations firm, and watching her develop

This book is about helping you find your first job.

her path and voice into the future of our business was also very revealing and helped shape this point of view.

Much of the advice in this book comes in the form of stories because it leverages eXploring as a technique. eXploring taught us the value of stories in helping our creative people to understand and internalize the truths of their audience. **The advice is designed to help you better understand how to approach your own job search in today's marketplace, give you very practical advice for breaking in, and prepare you for the kind of experiences you will have while you are working.** It will also help managers better understand the emerging workforce to ensure productivity and creativity. All the stories in this book are real people's stories but all the names have been changed. It isn't important who they are; it's only important that their stories resonate.

This book introduces a perspective about needing to find both your "path" and your "voice" over the course of your work life. **The "path" is the series of steps you take in your career. The "voice" is what you need if you are to find the career that is satisfying for you.** Newbies are very focused on their paths and what they need to do to get their first jobs. What they appreciate less is how important it is for a job to be the right fit and how useful it can be to take any job you can get as you work toward finding your voice.

In 30 years I have watched lots of people enter the advertising business. Today's generation of entry-level 20-somethings, the millennial cohorts Generation Y and Generation Z born sometime in the 1980s and 1990s, have some unique needs. There are lots of reasons why you need advice, but probably the most relevant one is that you are looking for work, and it is really tough out there right now. I'm not trying to write a sociological treatise about your generation's fundamental angst. I'm just trying to offer some suggestions that might help you get started.

The advertising business has grown tremendously in the past 50 years and, with **the dominance of the internet it has changed dramatically**. Advertising is attractive to many of you. It has lots of caché based on its inherent need for creativity. I decided to create this book as a way to help new graduates by borrowing from some of the experiences of new employees (those who have started working in the field in the past three years) and marrying them to the wisdom of the folks doing the hiring today.

The context

The context for this book is that new working people need to find their way through the job-search drama. You come out of school, aren't sure that you know what you want to "do with your life," and think you are supposed to know. You are anxious because **you think that you have to figure it out**

somehow BEFORE you start working. That you won't get a job unless you know what you want to "do" with the rest of your life. No wonder you are stressed. Imagine the pressure. If you don't get a job right away, if you aren't lucky enough to know you want to be a doctor or a lawyer or a teacher, you are terrified.

The challenge

Lots of young people are looking for work today. And these are challenging times. **The cohort graduating college and looking for work in advertising and marketing is larger than any since the famous post-World War II Baby Boom.** Make no mistake, the market is highly competitive. The group that tends to seek out advertising jobs has usually completed a four-year college program, and many of you have completed some remarkable internships or on-campus academic experiences in which you have created impressive looking advertising strategies and campaigns as part of your course work.

As someone who has read quite a few resumes in the last few years, I have found that many prospective candidates, even those from the most selective universities, don't always find it so easy to get jobs. **The hints in this book are about helping you find your first job.** My goal is to help you get started and feel a little less anxious while you are doing it.

I've noticed that many people who come to me in search of a start don't really understand what they should be asking themselves before they talk to me. They don't understand why I ask them whether they have ever held a job before. Or what it is they like to do on the weekends. Or even what their parents do for a living. I've witnessed that many new college graduates don't know how to think about finding a job, or even really understand what it means to look for one. **And the most important thing they don't understand is how they should think about their personal strengths. How they should best position themselves to find their way. How they should differentiate themselves to stand out and make it possible for me to help them.**

This isn't true only for account managers and strategists. Creative people too need to find an on-ramp beyond their portfolio "books." But just don't take my word for it. **Listen to the words of Diane Fields,** Creative Services Manager at Y&R as she describes how she interviews candidates:

Sure their book is important. But let's face it, they don't get to me without a strong book. I ask them to tell me about themselves. I try to find out what they will be like to work with, what makes them tick. If they can't describe the experience of creating their work it raises questions for me. First I wonder whether the work is truly their own and then equally important for me is my feeling about whether or not they will fit in. Whether people will want to work with them, whether they have the right genes for client service creativity. It's not enough to be talented. I need to know that they can use their talent in an organization. We can't do great work if we can't partner with clients in support of it. **I am looking for people with the right talent and the right personality. A winning combination.**

So you see, the on-ramp can be elusive. You can get close and still not find it.

But it's "so hard," you may say. "How do I know who I really am and who I am going to be when everything always changes, including me and the advertising business?"

I'm not unsympathetic. There is a very good chance that if you are young enough to need the lessons in this book you will live to be 100. So you are likely to be working for a good long time. The challenge of finding your first job can seem overwhelming, I suppose, if you think you are supposed to be finding the "thing" you want to do for the next 60 years, or as Princeton says in the Broadway hit *Avenue Q*, **your "purpose."** I understand the drama—graduating and leaving the comfortable university environment, finding a job, finding a place to live. And all when you are at a developmental stage, somewhere between teenager and adult. Of course there is a lot of tension and drama. I hope some of the words in this book will help you.

How you
want to
express
yourself in
your job is
your voice.

THE ABCs
A. Look for your path AND your voice

I've been asked for a lot of advice about getting started and time and again I feel I have been asked **the wrong question**.

Beginners always ask me about the best **path** to get started. But they never ask about **how to find their voice**. And the two are different—related but different. **Your path is how to get there.** One step, following the next. This major in school leads to this first job leads to this next job. So they think. And so new graduates ask questions about the **path**:

"Belle, what was your path?"

"What did you study?"

"What was your first job?"

"How did you get it?"

"Should I go to graduate school?"

"My uncle will give me a job, should I take it?"

But they never ask about **the voice!**

What is the voice?

Finding your voice is so much more satisfying (and I think so much more important as well as complicated) than finding your path. **The voice is how you want to express yourself in your job. What you want your expertise to be. The voice is all about the affinity and facility you will have in a job.** It is related to how the job sounds to you when you hear yourself talking about it, how it uses your skills, how you feel about it, whether it seems right for you, whether you care about the industry, or the issues in your work. **Your voice is about what you like to do in your spare time. It's about what turns you on, what really tickles you.** There are clues to your voice every step of the way, but new graduates don't look for them because they are very focused on the path. High school to college was a path so new graduates in this cohort have an expectation that this next stage in their lives has a path as well. But it isn't that simple.

Jobs are about fit! And *fit* is about your path AND your voice.

What can be tricky for new graduates is that both parts don't always grow at the same rate. But what can be liberating is that you need to be open to thinking about both when you look for your first job and if you are, then that first job can be easier to find. **If you are thinking about both, then it doesn't really matter what your first job is.**

If you take a first job and you like it, then you have taken your first step on the path. Lucky you. But the data collected for this book show that this rarely happens. What usually happens is that you take a first job, and the best thing you can say about it is that it got you your next job. But in truth it probably did something else too.

If you take a first job and don't like it, you have taken your first step toward finding your voice as well as the first step on the path. How wonderfully important! The interview for your second job will be so much better because you have something truthful to say about working. And the job will therefore be easier to get.

First, obviously, the interviewer for your second job will believe that you know what it means to work, to get there, to collaborate, to be part of a professional organization. But what you may not realize is that when you are asked why you are leaving you will have an answer that comes from the heart, and so that will really mean something to the interviewer. Whatever your first job is **you learn something about the business and about yourself and you can bring it to your next job.** I promise you will be much more valuable to your second employer than you are to your first.

So this means there should be less to worry about. Just get a job. Any job. And you are one step closer to your path AND your voice.

How I know

I'm pretty sure I never had a conscious path in my career. I do know that I found my voice by following my heart from one opportunity to the next. Here is my story:

I started looking for work as a French major with a master's degree in human psychological development from the Harvard Graduate School of Education, desperate to be anything other than a school teacher. I came from a long line of teachers on both sides of my family and in the newly emerging feminist era, I was desperate to do something else. The master's program appealed to me because the catalog explained that the professors had been responsible for the testing and creative research used to develop the just-launched program *Sesame Street*. I wanted to use my degree to make television programming to help kids. And so I signed up. Of course what it didn't say in the catalog was that upon graduating with my master's there would not likely be a job doing research for *Sesame Street* and that I would have to find some other work. Once I had my master's, I took a job with a research firm, specializing in testing children's commercials.

Thus I entered the world of marketing research, still unsure about how I would make my mark but excited to find a way to use what I knew and continue to learn. Rather than dwell on how many gigs I have had in my career, let me just say that **every time I felt I was no longer learning**

Worry more about your voice. Your path will follow.

and growing, or having a satisfying experience or being recognized appropriately (and paid fairly!), I moved on to another type of work—similar, related, but almost never by being promoted into my supervisor's job. When it could have been time to move up, I guess sometimes I simply moved on, following my voice, not an accepted path.

In the interests of full disclosure, I should say that I moved on within the same company. Shocking, I know. It was not typical in our industry even at that time, and probably not even possible today. But the fact is I was able to have a different kind of work experience, and the company changed so much (went from private to public, was bought out, developed some new lines of business and most importantly turned over its management so often that one could argue it became a new place) roughly every five years, so I didn't have to leave to move on.

I was happiest when my role let me do what it was I was good at—uncovering insights about consumers and how they feel about brands, collaborating with creative people about what new ads should say, doing research about why people behave the way they do. **I was happiest and most successful when the job I was paid to do let me express my "voice." Simple but true.** When you aren't feeling as though you are pretending to care, or have to behave in a certain way that doesn't feel natural to you, you are using your voice. Of course, all experiences, even difficult or unpleasant ones can contribute to your success because you increase your knowledge of the business and how to get things done. But what they really do is help you find and commit to your voice.

I was least happy at work when I got caught up in watching other people's career "paths." If you work in an organization, you tend to look around a lot and try to model your path on those of other people. Work went well for me when what the company needed me to do was something I was good at that really turned me on intellectually, when I was able to get passionate about the challenges I was facing. When I focused too much on whether what I was asked to do seemed like a plum assignment or whether someone else seemed to have a better job, work did not go as well. **I've learned that jobs are first and foremost about fit, and the only career path that matters is the one you follow to figure out what you are good at and what you like to do** while you are getting paid.

The secret of my success is that when I was really unhappy, I would find a way to learn and move on. Along the way, I became an expert. **I worried more about my voice; my path followed me. And, if you work at your voice, your path will follow as well.**

The care and feeding of ideas: from strategy to creative.

THE ABCs
B. Resilience and collaboration

Listen to a story about Anna. She worked nights and weekends at Bloomingdale's department store while going to college. After a long day of studying in a full-time university program, she had the poise and patience to wait on customers with a smile. Advertising is a service business. Our clients often call us with last-minute unreasonable requests. It is hard to keep smiling, hard to say "of course, client" when you don't feel that way. When I spoke to Anna about breaking into advertising she downplayed her current job. "It's just a sales job," she said. But when Anna told me about finding a dress for a woman in a size 12 by calling six other stores, I knew she was a young woman with the right kind of personality for our business.

It was when I asked her to tell me about what she liked about the job that **this story came out.** I didn't know the story so I would have no way of knowing how wonderfully diligent she is. My question wasn't, "Tell me about what you do at work, Anna," yet in a role-playing exercise she told it to me. And I'm glad she did. I would never have gotten there myself. And it would have been my loss. Of course, she is still a beginner. If I didn't have an entry-level opening, I would not call her in. But I see that she has worked. That she is determined and understands what it takes. **All she had to do was tell me how what she did at Bloomingdale's (sell clothes) is related to what I need her to do in an advertising job (push through our creative ideas) and she's got a story I want to hear.**

People breaking in may not be aware that identifying a sound strategy for a brand is only one piece of our jobs as advertising planners. **The care and feeding of ideas, moving from strategy to creative and helping to nurture good ideas, is a critical role for all agency professionals.** The ability to collaborate, to compromise and, of course, to communicate clearly to move things forward is prized in the business. Consultative selling, or the art of supporting your recommendations by taking the perspective of your audience is a core concept in the creation of effective advertising and equally as important for practitioners doing their jobs. **We have two audiences—our agencies as well as our clients—so the need for collaboration is heightened. We work in cross-disciplinary teams, which means we need to compromise before we even get our ideas out to our clients. It can be difficult.** We don't just figure out what to do, we have to get it done. Figuring it out is a small part. We need to bring our internal team along and then sell an idea to a client.

Zoe Church is a native Australian and Global Pitch Master responsible for coordinating major business development initiatives for Y&R. **Zoe says that when she talks to a candidate she is trying to determine whether or not the candidate is "someone I'd like to invite to a barbecue."** So much of what we do is done in teams and requires long hours. We don't want to hire people with whom we would prefer not to spend the afternoon.

Working in advertising is a marathon, not a sprint. You figure something out—for example, what an ad should say or what kind of recommendation is needed—then you need to get a creative team to execute, then you bring it to a client, then you revise it, then you re-present it to the client, then you revise it, then you produce it, then you test it, then you revise it yet again. You need patience. You need to be resilient. You need to be endlessly optimistic. If you try to go in one way and you can't, then you need to go another way. Figuring out what to do is a very small part of the process. **To be happy and successful in advertising you first need to be able to figure it out and then drag it along to get it sold.** Not everyone is good at everything but in this business **it helps if you find the collaboration as much fun as the thinking.**

This is where finding your voice can help. You might think you have the skills for a job but feel it just isn't for you.

Collaborate, compromise, and communicate clearly to move things forward.

Here is another story: There was a wonderful young man named Steve who worked for me who would do anything for me. He was eager, he was determined to get to a good answer. He was a brilliant, different kind of thinker. When our team had a question to answer, his answer always brought a new perspective. **He loved jumping in and out of projects, bringing new data and information. But he hated bringing the team along with him.** He hated having to change the wording of his recommendations simply because someone else believed that "it was clearer" that way, that the client would understand it better if it were reframed. He had trouble with the agency and client teams as a result. He argued when he was told to change something. He complained if the questions weren't clear. He just couldn't match his working style to the collaborative group style that was emerging at our agency. **His voice just wasn't right.** So he moved on, to a slot in a company that issued points of views and perspectives on people. That is what they were commissioned to do. At our agency he was a square peg trying to fit in a round hole. **He needed to shape his path around his voice.** He just didn't speak "collaboration" the way he needed to in order to be happy at our agency.

THE ABCs
C. The power of differentiation

Seth graduated from George Washington University. He was president of the advertising club, charismatic and energetic. He could talk quite passionately about the advertising business but was having trouble breaking in.

Lots of people who want to get into marketing come with beautiful credentials. But hidden in Seth's resume was the column he wrote on cars for the school newspaper. He was a car nut. **And it was the car nut that I could help. He had a focus that made him different from the "average above-average" applicant.** What his expertise in cars became was both **interesting and valuable,** especially to advertising agencies in Detroit who needed car people, even beginners.

Seth was open to working in Detroit because he loved cars. He had just never thought about using his hobby to build his career. But a point of difference like that can really help whoever is interviewing you understand whether there is a

The first thing a brand needs to do is establish its differentiated meaning.

place for you. If you have one, don't hide it. Bring it on, so you can help the interviewer help you find your voice, not just your path.

At Y&R our understanding of the power of differentiation comes from our proprietary brand equity model and knowledge source called **BrandAsset Valuator.**® For the past 20 years we have been studying what helps brands grow and thrive and we have proven empirically that the first thing a brand needs to do is establish its differentiated meaning. It's no different for you. **You are trying to build your personal brand, to make me understand why I should choose you over another applicant. I need to be able to index you in my archives and retrieve you when I have a need for someone like you.** Young people often think they need to make it clear that they are open to doing "anything" when they are trying to break in. Of course they are. It is expected. But what agencies need to know is how, if we hire you, you will be able to help us do what we need to do. **You need to sell me on your ability to help me do what I need to do.**

We recently hired an intern in our strategy department, Elizabeth from NYU, who came to us with a self-defined major on her transcript called "Psychographic Segmentation." I was intrigued by the notion of such a specialized major, one that seemed almost too specific for a university education. But it helped us notice her. It gave her something to talk about, why she chose it, what it meant to her and what she was learning.

It is interesting that in this case it was her academic grounding that drew her to us, but her performance as an intern is what made us want to help her once she graduated. She was diligent and self-possessed. Her major didn't matter.

You may think that finding your differentiation requires more understanding of business and interviewer needs than a beginner can have. But even if you feel that way, **the best way you can help yourself is to make your own personal differentiation clear. Tell me what turns you on, tell me what you have done, tell me with pride and confidence what you are good at. The better you do that, the better I will understand you and be able to envision you helping me do my thing.** The more I think you stand for something, the more I can imagine you being able to support the agency's initiatives. Of course the converse is also true. If I don't think you will fit but your strengths are clear, I may not be able to imagine you helping me but I will be much better able to make recommendations about where you might fit elsewhere.

This is very important. Young people are afraid to niche themselves and make themselves seem wrong for a slot. But **the lack of differentiation actually works against you.** If you seem too wishy-washy, I worry that I can't imagine you fitting in. Why do I need you? Why do my clients?

Why should I, or my colleagues, spend any time talking to you?

Your resume: bring me something I can use

There is no perfect resume. You don't need to worry about making one. You just need to create yours in a way that makes me, the interviewer, interested and opens the door to the conversation you really want us to have.

I'm certain you are going to get a lot of advice about your resume. All job hunters do. In my opinion a lot of that advice is not very helpful. Rather than talk about it theoretically, I want to offer some practical advice from the point of view of someone who has to use your resume to structure an interview.

A resume can't lose you a job, but it can lose you an interview. When I look at your resume I am looking to see if I should spend any of my time (or recommend that others in my company spend their time) talking to you. I expect you to look differentiated, determined, and collaborative. I want to think that I will enjoy talking to you. **The purpose of your resume is for you to enable a conversation with me about your strengths.**

I am going to use your resume to structure our conversation because, until you start talking, it may be all I know about you (as well as any insights I may have picked up checking out your Facebook page). But assume I'm busy and I am going to scan your resume as we talk to structure the interview. **Everything on your resume is fair game for our discussion. Everything!** If you don't want to talk about something, don't put it on your resume. You are just getting started. I don't want to see a chronology of how you have spent every moment of your young adult life. I want to see relevant things you have done. And you are the only one who knows if they are relevant— I don't because I don't know what you have done. If something is on your resume, you need to be prepared to talk about it in a way that sounds relevant to me. **Rehearse out loud,** in advance.

So here is a hint that most of the students with whom I've spoken have found very helpful:

When you write your resume you also need to think about the talking points you want to hit, the **talk track** you want to follow during our conversation.

Take a lesson from politicians, wonderful marketers all! Of course, I am going to have a few questions to ask you about advertising and why you think you want to do it and why you think you will be good at it. But no matter what I ask you, you need to be prepared with the things you want me to know about you when the interview is finished.

Structure your resume to make me ask you about stories you have prepared to tell me.

In Chapter 7, "The Talk Track," I will give you some questions I think you should be prepared to answer, but in terms of creating your resume, you want to structure it as much as you can to make me ask you about the stories you have prepared to tell me.

Resume Tips

Here are a few suggestions about how your resume should **look**, what it should **contain** and how it should be **organized**, so that it works hard on your behalf and the interviewer does not have to work too hard.

Your name at the top, of course—easy to read, in a large enough, bold enough font, saved in a .doc or .pdf file that is called "Anna" (your name) not simply "resume-1-2013." I get a lot of resumes. When I save them into a file, why should *I* have to retype *your* name (and how would I ever find you again if I forget to)? **And make sure it is easy to open.** Maybe avoid the newest software or the wildest font because if I can't open it, I may simply ignore it.

This doesn't mean I don't want you to make your resume look good. **Readability** and **emphasis** are the most important criteria. At the risk of sounding contradictory, several students have told me that the "Career Services" people at their college insist they use Times New Roman, perhaps because everyone can read it and the layout will be the same. I hate that font. It looks like old typewriter font to me. How old are those "Career Services" folks anyway and what is their career experience? I especially dislike the use of Times New Roman by people who are trying to get into a marketing communications agency. I am not suggesting that you never follow Career Services' advice. I am telling you that this is a creative business and that font is old-fashioned. Just pick something clean and clear that is big enough and fairly common.

(If you are still in school, and in order to graduate you have to prepare a resume for "Career Services," that seems very different from what I am describing here, feel free. But just be thankful for technology that enables you to **send the resume you want to send** *when you actually look for work!)*

What about an **objective?**

Yes, OK, if you are just starting out. But customize it to the job you are looking for. And identify strengths you want to use. An objective that says "I am looking to learn" makes me feel I need to teach you. Of course you are going to learn, you are a beginner. But tell me what it is about you that makes you a good person for me to want to teach. And if you are worried that these types of objectives sound dorky, just make sure it helps you differentiate yourself in a way that isn't pompous.

Your resume should be **ONE PAGE!**

You are just starting out. I would be very surprised if you need more than that to shape a discussion with me. **About 1/4 of the way down, what I like to call the "good real estate" on the page, is the thing you want me to ask you about most**—your most relevant job or internship, your current part-time job if you have one, and it should be spun to help me understand how great it would be for me to have you work with us.

And once you graduate college, I no longer care about **high school**

Unless you have some fabulous award, graduated first in your class, or went to a high school you think I may have gone to, I don't care about extracurricular activities exclusively from high school.

If you were the president of the social service club in high school, AND in college AND you currently tutor kids from underprivileged neighborhoods, then I do care about that side of you. I care a lot and expect it to be in the "Skills & Interests" section of your resume. It needs to be there as **a special quality you have,** NOT as a chronological reporting of what you have done.

Your job is not to show me you are well-rounded. Your job is to show me your personal differentiation.

What is it that makes you who you are and will help me see how wonderful it would be to have you as part of our organization?

A lot of this may seem obvious, but let me assure you that I get many resumes that don't conform and that make me work harder than I want to in order to figure out if I am interested in an applicant.

Take a look at Anna's two resumes

I've already introduced you to Anna. She is a wonderfully vivacious young woman with great energy and presence. At first meeting you want to like her and thus hire her if you can. But as I explained earlier, I really had to dig to find some experience that seemed relevant to me based on the first resume she sent.

The next several pages are a section-by-section look at Anna's two resumes with the suggestions I made to her.

You can see that some are subtle and others more substantive. My overarching point of view was that much of what I really would have wanted to hear about was **too hidden** in her original document. Remember, an entry-level interviewer doesn't generally spend a lot of time with your resume and doesn't want to work that hard to figure out what you are bringing to the party. **You need to know what your strengths are and figure out a way to help the interviewer ask you about them.** **The resume is the first step.**

anna's resume

This one is basically upside-down

• Small, low-impact font

Anna R. Santiago
226 Manor House Dr. Apt. K-11
Haworth, NJ 07641
ars25@CNA.edu - xxx-xxx-xxxx

OBJECTIVE:	To obtain an internship in magazine publishing that will enhance my academic and professional experience.
EDUCATION:	**The College of New Amsterdam**

BA in Communication
Expected Graduation, December 2009
Specialization: Advertising/Public Relations
Minor: Journalism

• All about school

Related Course Work:
Introduction to Journalism/Reporting and Writing 1/Radio Journalism/
Introduction to Public Relations/ Public Relations Writing/ Introduction to
Advertising/ Advertising Management 1

EXPERIENCE:

Fall 2007- Current — **_The Campus_, College and Harlem Community Newspaper**
Contributing writer: 'Arts and Entertainment'
"Documenting Dominicans in New York", "Global City Hosts
New Amsterdam Professors", "Graduate Center: Chamber Concert"
"What Are Your Favorite Weekend Activities?"—Feature
Articles posted on: _www.myspace.com/myvoicecarries_

11/2007-Current — **Bloomingdales, White Plains, NY**
Sales Associate
• Drive sales in the department through outstanding customer service

9/2004-Current — **Caperberry Events, White Plains, NY**
Banquet Waitress
• Assist in supervision of waitresses
• Focus on customer satisfaction during events

•**Dates** take priority over the **activities** she wants me to know about

6/2003-8/2006 — **American Leisure, Nanuet, NY**
Head Lifeguard
• Completed payroll, managed weekly schedules and hired lifeguards, supervised four lifeguards

SKILLS: — Microsoft Word, PowerPoint, Excel
Creative: writing, drawing – portfolio available
Fluent Spanish, conversational Italian

Now look at the second version:

anna's resume 2.0

Anna R. Santiago
226 Manor House Dr. Apt. K-11
Haworth, NJ 07641
ar.santiago@gmail.com - xxx-xxx-xxxx

• Her **name stands out,** as does the fact . . .

OBJECTIVE   Implement my strengths in organization, collaboration and communication to obtain an entry level position in account management at Young & Rubicam.

EDUCATION   The College of New Amsterdam, BA Media and Communication Arts
Expected Graduation: **December 2009**
Specialization: Advertising/Public Relations. Minor: Journalism

EXPERIENCE

| Bloomingdale's | Sales Associate | 11/2007-Current | White Plains, NY |

- Drive sales in the department through outstanding customer service
- Incorporate consumer insight when rearranging product displays to improve sales of new merchandise
- Use intranet program to add customers to client lists for future calls regarding private events

. . . that she holds a part-time job while in school.

| Caperberry Events | Banquet Waitress | 9/2004-Current | White Plains, NY |

- Assist maitre d' in supervision of 10-15 staff throughout event
- Integrate my creative skills in putting together visually appealing food stations
- Support customer satisfaction initiatives during events by ensuring staff preparedness

| American Leisure | Head Lifeguard | 6/2003-8/2006 | Nanuet, NY |

- Supervised 5 lifeguards, managed schedules, completed payroll, recruited and trained new staff

| The Campus Newspaper | Writer | Fall 2007-Current | New York, NY |

- *www.internetaddress.com/myvoicecarries*
- Contribute stories and features to Arts and Entertainment section
- Research stories pertinent to the college and the Harlem Community

SKILLS AND INTERESTS

- Flexibility, interpersonal ability, multi-tasking, creativity
- Fluent Spanish, conversational Italian
- Microsoft Office
- Cooking with salsa

I am able to see that she is an active young woman who understands what work means. Of course I am going to ask her about her jobs—**look at where they are located on her resume**—and she is going to have great stories to tell me about how diligent an employee she is, which will be **relevant** to me.

anna's resume

Move beyond your school email address

- Think about an email address with your name, to help me remember.

Anna R. Santiago
226 Manor House Dr. Apt. K-11
Haworth, NJ 07641
ars25@CNA.edu - xxx-xxx-xxxx

OBJECTIVE:
To obtain an internship in magazine publishing that will enhance my academic and professional experience.

EDUCATION:
The College of New Amsterdam
BA in Communication
Expected Graduation, December 2009
Specialization: Advertising/Public Relations
Minor: Journalism

Related Course Work:
Introduction to Journalism/Reporting and Writing 1/Radio Journalism/ Introduction to Public Relations/ Public Relations Writing/ Introduction to Advertising/ Advertising Management 1

EXPERIENCE:

Fall 2007- Current
The Campus, College and Harlem Community Newspaper
Contributing writer: 'Arts and Entertainment'
"Documenting Dominicans in New York", "Global City Hosts New Amsterdam Professors", "Graduate Center: Chamber Concert"
"What Are Your Favorite Weekend Activities?"—Feature
Articles posted on: *www.myspace.com/myvoicecarries*

11/2007-Current
Bloomingdales, White Plains, NY
Sales Associate
- Drive sales in the department through outstanding customer service

9/2004-Current
Caperberry Events, White Plains, NY
Banquet Waitress
- Assist in supervision of waitresses
- Focus on customer satisfaction during events

6/2003-8/2006
American Leisure, Nanuet, NY
Head Lifeguard
- Completed payroll, managed weekly schedules and hired lifeguards, supervised four lifeguards

SKILLS:
Microsoft Word, PowerPoint, Excel
Creative: writing, drawing – portfolio available
Fluent Spanish, conversational Italian

Font is cleaner and more contemporary

Anna R. Santiago
226 Manor House Dr. Apt. K-11
Haworth, NJ 07641
ar.santiago@gmail.com - xxx-xxx-xxxx

• Slightly **bump up** the size of your name.

OBJECTIVE   Implement my strengths in organization, collaboration and communication to obtain an entry level position in account management at Young & Rubicam.

EDUCATION   The College of New Amsterdam, BA Media and Communication Arts
Expected Graduation: **December 2009**
Specialization: Advertising/Public Relations. Minor: Journalism

EXPERIENCE

Bloomingdales   Sales Associate   11/2007-Current   White Plains, NY
- Drive sales in the department through outstanding customer service
- Incorporate consumer insight when rearranging product displays to improve sales of new merchandise
- Use intranet program to add customers to client lists for future calls regarding private events

Caperberry Events   Banquet Waitress   9/2004-Current   White Plains, NY
- Assist maitre d' in supervision of 10-15 staff throughout event
- Integrate my creative skills in putting together visually appealing food stations
- Support customer satisfaction initiatives during events by ensuring staff preparedness

American Leisure   Head Lifeguard   6/2003-8/2006   Nanuet, NY
- Supervised 5 lifeguards, managed schedules, completed payroll, recruited and trained new staff

The Campus Newspaper   Writer   Fall 2007-Current   New York, NY
- *www.internetaddress.com/myvoicecarries*
- Contribute stories and features to Arts and Entertainment section
- Research stories pertinent to the college and the Harlem Community

SKILLS AND INTERESTS
- Flexibility, interpersonal ability, multi-tasking, creativity
- Fluent Spanish, conversational Italian
- Microsoft Office
- Cooking with salsa

Your name is more important than the rest of the info and should stand out.

anna's resume

Think about a bit more **sell copy** that focuses on your strengths and "ask for the order."

Anna R. Santiago
226 Manor House Dr. Apt. K-11
Haworth, NJ 07641
ars25@CNA.edu - xxx-xxx-xxxx

OBJECTIVE: To obtain an internship in magazine publishing that will enhance my academic and professional experience.

EDUCATION: The College of New Amsterdam
BA in Communication
Expected Graduation, December 2009
Specialization: Advertising/Public Relations
Minor: Journalism

Related Course Work:
Introduction to Journalism/Reporting and Writing 1/Radio Journalism/
Introduction to Public Relations/ Public Relations Writing/ Introduction to
Advertising/ Advertising Management 1

EXPERIENCE:

Fall 2007- Current *The Campus*, College and Harlem Community Newspaper
Contributing writer: 'Arts and Entertainment'
"Documenting Dominicans in New York", "Global City Hosts
New Amsterdam Professors", "Graduate Center: Chamber Concert"
"What Are Your Favorite Weekend Activities?"—Feature
Articles posted on: *www.myspace.com/myvoicecarries*

11/2007-Current **Bloomingdales, White Plains, NY**
Sales Associate
• Drive sales in the department through outstanding customer service

9/2004-Current **Caperberry Events, White Plains, NY**
Banquet Waitress
• Assist in supervision of waitresses
• Focus on customer satisfaction during events

6/2003-8/2006 **American Leisure, Nanuet, NY**
Head Lifeguard
• Completed payroll, managed weekly schedules and hired lifeguards,
supervised four lifeguards

SKILLS: Microsoft Word, PowerPoint, Excel
Creative: writing, drawing – portfolio available
Fluent Spanish, conversational Italian

Anna R. Santiago
226 Manor House Dr. Apt. K-11
Haworth, NJ 07641
ar.santiago@gmail.com - xxx-xxx-xxxx

OBJECTIVE Implement my strengths in organization, collaboration and
communication to obtain an entry level position in account management
at Young & Rubicam.

EDUCAT   m, BA Media and Communication Arts

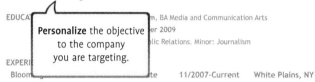

Personalize the objective to the company you are targeting.

er 2009

blic Relations. Minor: Journalism

EXPERI

Bloom   te   11/2007-Current   White Plains, NY
- Drive sales in the department through outstanding customer service
- Incorporate consumer insight when rearranging product displays to improve sales of new merchandise
- Use intranet program to add customers to client lists for future calls regarding private events

Caperberry Events   Banquet Waitress   9/2004-Current   White Plains, NY
- Assist maitre d' in supervision of 10-15 staff throughout event
- Integrate my creative skills in putting together visually appealing food stations
- Support customer satisfaction initiatives during events by ensuring staff preparedness

American Leisure   Head Lifeguard   6/2003-8/2006   Nanuet, NY
- Supervised 5 lifeguards, managed schedules, completed payroll, recruited and trained new staff

The Campus Newspaper Writer   Fall 2007-Current   New York, NY
- *www.internetaddress.com/myvoicecarries*
- Contribute stories and features to Arts and Entertainment section
- Research stories pertinent to the college and the Harlem Community

SKILLS AND INTERESTS
- Flexibility, interpersonal ability, multi-tasking, creativity
- Fluent Spanish, conversational Italian
- Microsoft Office
- Cooking with salsa

A lot of beginners talk about leadership. But really I don't expect you to be a leader. I want you to be a partner. Subtle difference but important when you are starting out. Talk like a leader about how well you **collaborate**.

anna's resume

Anna R. Santiago
226 Manor House Dr. Apt. K-11
Haworth, NJ 07641
ars25@CNA.edu - xxx-xxx-xxxx

> Shorten the block of education.

To obtain an internship in magazine publishing that will enhance my academic and professional experience.

EDUCATION:

The College of New Amsterdam
BA in Communication
Expected Graduation, December 2009
Specialization: Advertising/Public Relations
Minor: Journalism

> • It's OK to include course work. Just not a lot and not if it is repetitive.

Related Course Work:
Introduction to Journalism/Reporting and Writing 1/Radio Journalism/
Introduction to Public Relations/ Public Relations Writing/ Introduction to
Advertising/ Advertising Management 1

EXPERIENCE:

Fall 2007- Current
The Campus, College and Harlem Community Newspaper
Contributing writer: 'Arts and Entertainment'
"Documenting Dominicans in New York", "Global City Hosts
New Amsterdam Professors", "Graduate Center: Chamber Concert"
"What Are Your Favorite Weekend Activities?"—Feature
Articles posted on: *www.myspace.com/myvoicecarries*

11/2007-Current
Bloomingdales, White Plains, NY
Sales Associate
• Drive sales in the department through outstanding customer service

9/2004-Current
Caperberry Events, White Plains, NY
Banquet Waitress
• Assist in supervision of waitresses
• Focus on customer satisfaction during events

6/2003-8/2006
American Leisure, Nanuet, NY
Head Lifeguard
• Completed payroll, managed weekly schedules and hired lifeguards,
supervised four lifeguards

SKILLS:
Microsoft Word, PowerPoint, Excel
Creative: writing, drawing – portfolio available
Fluent Spanish, conversational Italian

> If you say you majored in advertising/public relations with a minor in journalism I would expect you to have those courses so don't waste space. I'm not the university registrar checking the prerequisites.

anna's resume 2.0

Anna R. Santi[ago]
226 Manor House Dr.
Haworth, NJ 07[0]
ar.santiago@gmail.com - xx

> Make sure the important thing—the date you are available, your **graduation date**—is obvious to me.

OBJECTIVE   Implement my strengths in organization, [col]laboration and communication to obtain an entry level position in account management at Young & Rubicam.

EDUCATION   The College of New Amsterdam, BA Media and Communication Arts
Expected Graduation: **December 2009**
Specialization: Advertising/Public Relations. Minor: Journalism

EXPERIENCE

Bloomingdales   Sales Associate   11/2007-Current   White Plains, NY
- Drive sales in the department through outstanding customer service
- Incorporate consumer insight when rearranging product displays to improve sales of new merchandise
- Use intranet program to add customers to client lists for future calls regarding private events

Caperberry Events   Banquet Waitress   9/2004-Current   White Plains, NY
- Assist maitre d' in supervision of 10-15 staff throughout event
- Integrate my creative skills in putting together visually appealing food stations
- Support customer satisfaction initiatives during events by ensuring staff preparedness

American Leisure   Head Lifeguard   6/2003-8/2006   Nanuet, NY
- Supervised 5 lifeguards, managed schedules, completed payroll, recruited and trained new staff

The Campus Newspaper   Writer   Fall 2007-Current   New York, NY
- www.internetaddress.com/myvoicecarries
- Contribute stories and features to Arts and Entertainment section
- Research stories pertinent to the college and the Harlem Community

SKILLS AND INTERESTS
- Flexibility, interpersonal ability, multi-tasking, creativity
- Fluent Spanish, conversational Italian
- Microsoft Office
- Cooking with salsa

> The "**good real estate**" on the page is the thing you want me to ask you about **most**. If you are looking for your first job it is OK to give education the "good real estate," just don't use it all up.

anna's resume

Less-relevant summer jobs should be there to show industriousness, but they should take up **less room**.

Anna R. Santiago
226 Manor House Dr. Apt. K-11
Haworth, NJ 07641
ars25@CNA.edu - xxx-xxx-xxxx

OBJECTIVE: To obtain an internship in magazine publishing that will enhance my academic and professional experience.

EDUCATION: The College of New Amsterdam
BA in Communication
Expected Graduation, December 2009
Specialization: Advertising/Public Relations
Minor: Journalism

Related Course Work:
Introduction to Journalism/Reporting and Writing 1/Radio Journalism/
Introduction to Public Relations/ Public Relations Writing/ Introduction to
Advertising/ Advertising Management 1

Worry less about **chronology** and more about **job relevance**.

EXPERIENCE:

Fall 2007- Current **The Campus, College and Harlem Community Newspaper**
Contributing writer: 'Arts and Entertainment'
"Documenting Dominicans in New York", "Global City Hosts
New Amsterdam Professors", "Graduate Center: Chamber Concert"
"What Are Your Favorite Weekend Activities?"—Feature
Articles posted on: *www.myspace.com/myvoicecarries*

11/2007-Current **Bloomingdales, White Plains, NY**
Sales Associate
• Drive sales in the department through outstanding customer service

9/2004-Current **Caperberry Events, White Plains, NY**
Banquet Waitress
• Assist in supervision of waitresses
• Focus on customer satisfaction during events

6/2003-8/2006 **American Leisure, Nanuet, NY**
Head Lifeguard
• Completed payroll, managed weekly schedules and hired lifeguards,
supervised four lifeguards

SKILLS: Microsoft Word, PowerPoint, Excel
Creative: writing, drawing – portfolio available
Fluent Spanish, conversational Italian

It is good to link to a newsletter or paper or something you have written. Just make sure it is a **working link** and the **content** is something you want me to see. This is true for blogs and Twitter handles as well.

Anna R. Santiago
226 Manor House Dr. Apt. K-11
Haworth, NJ 07641
ar.santiago@gmail.com - xxx-xxx-xxxx

OBJECTIVE Implement my strengths in organization, collaboration and communication to obtain an entry level position in account management at Young & Rubicam.

EDUCATION The College of New Amsterdam, BA Media and Communication Arts
Expected Graduation: December 2009
Specialization: Advertising/Public Relations. Minor: Journalism

EXPERIENCE

Bloomingdale's   **Sales Associate**   **11/2007-Current**   **White Plains, NY**
- Drive sales in the department through outstanding customer service
- Incorporate consumer insight when rearranging product displays to improve sales of new merchandise
- Use intranet program to add customers to client lists for future calls regarding private events

Caperberry Events   **Banquet Waitress**   **9/2004-Current**   **White Plains, NY**
- Assist maitre d' in supervision of 10-15 staff throughout event
- Integrate my creative skills in putting together visually appealing food stations
- Support customer satisfaction initiatives during events by ensuring staff preparedness

American Leisure   **Head Lifeguard**   **6/2003-8/2006**   **Nanuet, NY**
- Supervised 5 lifeguards, managed schedules, completed payroll, recruited and trained new staff

The Campus Newspaper   **Writer**   **Fall 2007-Current**   **New York, NY**
- *www.internetaddress.com/myvoicecarries*
- Contribute stories and features to Arts and Entertainment section
- Research stories pertinent to the college and the Harlem Community

SKILLS AN

Sales is GREAT experience for our business. Bloomingdale's is a big brand and the fact that you are working while going to school is impressive. And by the way, for a person looking to work in marketing communications, having a brand like Bloomingdale's on your resume is a great thing. It's not just that many of your interviewers probably shop there and so will have opinions about the store, the brand itself is something you must be prepared to talk about. No matter what kind of job you have while in school, if you are working for a branded company, you can talk about branding with me in a way someone else can't. And you should be ready to do so.

65

anna's resume

Anna R. Santiago
226 Manor House Dr. Apt. K-11
Haworth, NJ 07641
ars25@CNA.edu - xxx-xxx-xxxx

OBJECTIVE: To obtain an internship in magazine publishing that will enhance my academic and professional experience.

EDUCATION: **The College of New Amsterdam**
BA in Communication
Expected Graduation, December 2009
Specialization: Advertising/Public Relations
Minor: Journalism

Related Course Work:
Introduction to Journalism/Reporting and Writing 1/Radio Journalism/
Introduction to Public Relations/ Public Relations Writing/ Introduction to
Advertising/ Advertising Management 1

EXPERIENCE:

Fall 2007- Current   ***The Campus*, College and Harlem Community Newspaper**
Contributing writer: 'Arts and Entertainment'
"Documenting Dominicans in New York", "Global City Hosts
New Amsterdam Professors", "Graduate Center: Chamber Concert"
"What Are Your Favorite Weekend Activities?"—Feature
Articles posted on: *www.myspace.com/myvoicecarries*

11/2007-Current   **Bloomingdales, White Plains, NY**
Sales Associate
• Drive sales in the department through

9/2004-Current   **Caperberry Events, White Pla**
Banquet Waitress
• Assist in supervision of waitres
• Focus on customer satisfaction during

> Remember,
> everything here is fair game—
> only put things you want
> me to know.

6/2003-8/2006   **American Leisure, Nanuet, NY**
Head Lifeguard
• Completed payroll, managed weekly schedules and hired lifeguards,
supervised four lifeguards

SKILLS: Microsoft Word, PowerPoint, Excel
Creative: writing, drawing – portfolio available
Fluent Spanish, conversational Italian

> I wouldn't focus on the
> portfolio unless you want
> to go into the creative
> department.

66

anna's resume 2.0

Anna R. Santiago
226 Manor House Dr. Apt. K-11
Haworth, NJ 07641
ar.santiago@gmail.com - xxx-xxx-xxxx

OBJECTIVE Implement my strengths in organization, collaboration and communication to obtain an entry level position in account management at Young & Rubicam.

EDUCATION The College of New Amsterdam, BA Media and Communication Arts
Expected Graduation: December 2009
Specialization: Advertising/Public Relations. Minor: Journalism

EXPERIENCE

Bloomingdales   Sales Associate   11/2007-Current   White Plains, NY
- Drive sales in the department through outstanding customer service
- Incorporate consumer insight when rearranging product displays to improve sales of new merchandise
- Use intranet program to add customers to client lists for future calls regarding private events

Caperberry Events   Banquet Waitress   9/2004-Current   White Plains, NY
- Assist maitre d' in supervision of 10-15 staff throughout event
- Integrate my creative skills in putting together visually appealing food stations
- Support customer satisfaction initiatives during events by ensuring staff preparedness

American Leisure   Head Lifeguard   6/2003-8/2006   Nanuet, NY
- Supervised 5 lifeguards, managed schedules, completed payroll, recruited and trained new staff

The Campus Newspaper   Writer   Fall 2007-Current   New York, NY
- *www.internetaddress.com/myvoicecarries*
- Contribute stories and features to Arts and Entertainment section
- Research stories pertinent to the college and the Harlem Community

SKILLS AND INTERESTS
- Flexibility, interpersonal ability, multi-tasking, creativity
- Fluent Spanish, conversational Italian
- Microsoft Office
- Cooking with salsa

I want to know that you are a hard worker who is also fun to be around, so some personal details are always good.

67

One more thing about resumes

One final hint that I'm sure is obvious to some of you is that **you can have more than ONE resume.** If you take to heart what I said about the interviewer using the resume to structure the conversation then it may be smart for you to tailor your resume for the interview you want to have. I believe you should interview for all sorts of jobs when you are first starting out so you can practice thinking about the different jobs, from the different points of view of the various interviewers. Following this logic, depending on what is on your resume, you would create a different version for a more sales-oriented slot than you would for a more research-oriented slot.

I get the sense that some of the blame here goes to the placement offices at universities. Many are so formulaic in their approach to student resumes that I wonder if the candidates become so stressed out about making a single perfect resume they don't want to have to think about making more than one. But it is not in your best interest to feel like that. **If you do your homework, and research the company, it will pay back.**

Research for the resume?

Often beginners don't have a good sense of the different parts of the advertising business. But in today's world of LinkedIn, it is easy to do enough homework to make some guesses about **which of your experiences you should focus on,** based on what you think your interviewer needs. It seems pretty logical to me that you could have a reason to edit your objective or put your in-school television internship higher up on the page than you might based on its chronological order, if you are seeing someone who is in the production department. Unfortunately, I see many resumes that are **simply a list of what candidates have done with no reflection of my priorities.** Lest you think I am suggesting you mis-represent what you have done, it should go without saying that I am NOT telling you that at all. But this is the marketing business and I am asking you to **apply some of its principles to marketing yourself.** It is amazing how much more interesting and memorable an interview becomes if something I am told is in sync with my needs. And I want to be able to go back and easily find the place on the resume that got us talking about it.

When I speak at universities, I am often asked if employers check out students on social media. I can honestly tell you yes, but personally, I do so in a haphazard fashion. But this should be a two-way street. You should be checking me out, too. Another thing I can tell you honestly is that I can count on my fingers the number of people who have done a good job researching me and trying to match what they tell me on their resumes to something I care about. The professional connections of your interviewer are much easier to find than they used to be. **Use information wisely when you construct your door-opening resume.**

Importantly, there is another reason we expect our candidates to **understand social media. We use it as a marketing channel for our clients. We are looking for candidates who really understand it** so they are able to apply their knowledge to the work they do for us. While we are not hiring you expecting you to have a wealth of experience, **a facility for and appreciation of the tools of advertising is becoming a must-have.**

A recent intern at Y&R studying at CCNY in the AD/PR program commented:

> Most of the communications textbooks and readings that are assigned in school were written decades ago; a time when social media was non-existent and the World Wide Web was only a seed of what it is today. Interning at an actual agency proved to be more valuable than all the textbook knowledge I had ingested over the course of my college career.

Try to think about this when you are interviewing for your first job. **In general we are interested in how you think** and **how you work, more than we are interested in what you know.** That isn't to say we don't care if you can learn, but we don't want to hire you for your leadership experience; **we want to hire you for how you can help us.**

When it comes to social media, young people are expected to be at the forefront of its use and **demonstrating mastery** over it should help you work your way in. If we can find **some embarrassing information about you without looking too hard,** then we know **you aren't really on top of the social media channel.** It may not be fun to think you have to worry about who can see your photos, but a dynamic social media presence that demonstrates how facile you are in the space can only help you as you look for the on-ramp.

The Talk Track
Preparing for and managing interviews

Your **talk track** consists of the points you want to make. The one or two things you need interviewers to remember about you. The things that make you different from everyone else I am seeing and the things that allow you to illustrate your differentiated themes as well as your resilience and collaboration. But don't worry. I don't expect the stories you tell me to be remarkable. I am not saying that unless you have published your thesis or won *American Idol* that I won't remember you. **Speak with passion** and try to make our conversation **real and personal** so I remember it and don't confuse you with someone else.

Now you are probably thinking you aren't in charge of what gets asked in an interview. And that is true to a certain extent. But actually **you need to practice what the politicos do. Stay on message. Answer my question but quickly move to your talk track.** If I say, "Why do you want to be in this business?" you need to answer me, but you really need to answer me with **an illustration of why you would be good at it.** You want to answer my question and then elaborate by linking the question to what you want me to know about you.

Without meeting you I can't tell you what your talk track needs to be. Yours is different from everyone else's. Yours is about you. But I know you have one. And I am pretty sure I could help you find yours if I spent some time with you. The trick here is that unless I already know you, you are going to have to find your talk track without my help.

Think about the things your friends and family know and love about you—not the ones that have to do with partying, unless you are looking for work as a party planner. **I want to hear about what makes you reliable, competent, and fun to work with. Why do I want you in my "lifeboat?" The interviewer's subtext in most interviews is, "Do I want to work with you? Do you seem eager and capable and fun?" You need to somehow convince me that I do want to work with you, because you are eager, capable, and fun.** Even if I have told you that we don't have any openings at this moment, that there is no specific job slot we are discussing, if you stay on message, when I next have an opening, I will know why I need you.

A lot of college kids tell me they are reluctant to "sell" themselves. Somehow they feel as though they are being less than honest when they do so. But if you don't, who will? I am not asking you to fake it. In fact, I am asking you to tell me

the truth about who you are and what you are good at.
This isn't about giving me answers I want to hear. It is about
telling me how you can help me. One of the
hardest things for beginners to do is put themselves in the
interviewer's shoes. So since you can't really do that, just tell
me who you really are and why I want to work with you. And
one last thought, just as with the resume, you might want to
have one or two talk tracks depending on the interviewer, the
company, and the nature of the job.

After you develop your talk track, **the most important
thing you can do for yourself is** practice. **Practice out
loud, with someone you know who has some experience
interviewing.** It doesn't have to be an advertising person.
You just need someone willing to rehearse with you who has
some skill at getting you to talk about yourself. Since you are
a beginner in our business, I am much more likely to want to
learn about you and how you think than I am to want to test
you about what you know. If you can make a personable, logical argument for why I should want to work with you, you will
have a much better chance of convincing me to hire you.

The Courtesy Interview: What and why?

This is an important step that happens a lot in today's competitive and highly networked world. Undoubtedly, as part of
your search you will run into a courtesy interview. Before we
go any further, let's just be sure we agree on what the courtesy interview is. Sometimes called an informational interview,

it generally happens when someone agrees to see you, but for no specific job. Maybe you have an "in" from a professor, or a friend of your mother, or someone who graduated from your college program the year before you. In fact, many times people agree to see you when there are no jobs. Is it worth going? Of course. Very much so.

Here's why. **You get to meet someone at a real company.** How exciting. But the interviewer has only agreed to it for "informational purposes" or as a "courtesy" to the person who arranged it. So how should you think about it and how should you prepare?

I am unequivocal about this. **You have one mission. The purpose of your courtesy interview is to get another interview.** If you walk out without one then in some sense you have **squandered** the chance. Most young people who come in call the courtesy interview an informational interview, and so they use it to get information about the industry, or the company. That's a fine topic of conversation during the interview but it can't be your only purpose. Think about it this way. You need to make an impression so that even if I have no job, I think of you when one opens up. Or when a colleague asks me if I know anyone, I think of you. **Finding your first job is a process, and it happens over time and several appointments. The courtesy interview is just a first step.**

Here's an approach. Since you have developed your talk track while preparing your resume, why not use the interview

to try it out? When the courtesy interviewer tells you something about his or her job, try to fit it to something you were
thinking about as part of your talk track.

Do you know the difference between **open-ended questions
and closed-ended questions**? It's like short answers and essay
questions on exams. Besides, "no thank you, I don't care for
anything to drink," if I have offered you something, **you want
to try to turn all questions you are asked into open-ended
questions. Even if they sound like a "yes" or a "no" will do,
figure out a way to talk more.** I once had a candidate
respond to the request for a bottle of water by asking me what
brand it was. That was a pretty cool move. We instantly got into
a conversation about the brilliant marketing that had built the
bottled water category. And I loved the chance to listen to her
profess brand preference for water. She got what brands are
about and I could tell. Take every opportunity to talk more!

Interviewing someone who doesn't talk much is hard work
for an interviewer. As a candidate you should try to **make
yourself easy to talk to.** Actually, when it comes to the
courtesy interview, it makes sense to approach it the way
you would **a very important get-acquainted conversation.**
You want to get to know me and **you want me to feel like
I know you.** For one thing, it may be that there are actually
jobs but I just didn't want to mention that to you before I
met you. But additionally, of course, **you never know when
something might open up.** If you make it easy for me to
talk to you, I will certainly feel better about hearing from

you at a later time when **there might be a real opening.**

You also need to **make it easy** for the courtesy interviewer **to help you.** By telling me things about yourself during our conversation, you have helped me help you in several ways. First, as I've said, a one-way chat is hard for me. If I am doing all the talking, that is no fun. Second, you should assume that I am at least somewhat inclined to try to help you, right? I have agreed to the interview after all, either because I am doing our shared contact a favor or I am helping my *alma mater* or something like that. So **the more you tell me, the more something might strike me about you that makes you useful to me** or to someone else I know. That would be a win-win. I agreed to help, and now you have said something that makes me think you might be right for something a friend of mine needs. How great would that be? I don't have something for you but I offer you **a chance to meet someone else.**

That's a very desirable outcome. Not only have I done a favor for someone I like, but I might be able to help another person I like. You come into a courtesy interview to start a relationship and to try to keep it going. Remember that **this is a journey to your path and your voice,** and you are at the beginning. Take it one step at a time.

Research again?

If you thought research was a one time activity, think again. You did it before you sent out your resume but it is even more critical once you've gotten someone to agree to meet with you. Learn about the company and the people you will meet. **Come prepared to ask questions.** Social media is a marketing competency of the future and I am astounded by the number of candidates who don't leverage it. **I expect you to come knowing something about me.** Either because you found someone I'm linked to or read my published interviews or articles, or checked into my professional affiliations. I would even be impressed if you knew something about my peers at other agencies. **At a minimum, ask me questions about the kinds of issues facing someone in my job.** Guess if you have to. You can reframe the questions based on my answer. Here is something obvious. I'm a consumer insights expert. It's in my title. Ask me about consumer trends you've read about in *USA Today.* **Just show me you are capable and curious.** It's worth it. I will be more engaged in the interview if I don't have to work hard to conduct it. It will tell me something about you. But more importantly, **you will find it hard to be successful in marketing if you can't master marketing yourself.** So give it a go.

After the interview

One last thought about interviewing. **You need to follow up with a thank-you.** While there are people who would advise you to do a handwritten card, in today's world I think an email is fine. **A cordial, short, personal and specific thank-you note.** I've heard stories from interviewers about receiving notes addressed to interviewers from other agencies. Be careful. Don't just write "thanks for your time and I really think I would like to work at (insert agency name here)." I need to feel the note didn't come out of a textbook. Remind me of something specific we spoke about. I don't want to make it sound like you won't get the job if you don't or that you will certainly get it if you do, but it is important to thank the interviewer for his or her time.

You especially want to **follow up with an email** if the interviewer has said that he or she has some thoughts for other people for you to meet. Just do it. Send the email. **The pressure is on you to be the one following up. You are the one who is looking for a job.** Resend the resume and remind me of our discussion. Ask specifically about anything I may have said I would do. Be a nudge. I won't think less of you. Remember I am a working person who is thinking about myself, about all the other things I have to do in a day; I am not thinking only about helping you. **So take the initiative, refresh my memory.** You won't be bothering me. If you don't hear from me, it won't be because you "annoyed" me by following up. There are lots of real reasons I might not get back to you exactly when I said I would. Maybe the budgets were cut and I didn't know it when we met. Or maybe what I said I would do simply slipped my mind. There are no guarantees when it comes to interview promises, and there is no harm in reaching out once or even twice after we have met. It's on you. Good luck.

Courtesy Interview Checklist

Before

- ✓ Prepare Your Talk Track
- ✓ Rehearse Out Loud
- ✓ Stay on Message

During

- ✓ Talk About Yourself
- ✓ Help the Interviewer Help You
- ✓ Find a Way to Get Another Interview

After

- ✓ Say Thank You
- ✓ Follow Up on Your Next Appointment
- ✓ **Repeat!**

Your first job

It's very hard to transition from school to work. Listen to the story of **Pamela,** a junior at the College of the Holy Cross. A high-achieving student, Pamela had a successful internship at Y&R for the summer before her senior year and was quite honest about **her ambivalence and her anxiety about beginning her job search** for real:

> I have completely mixed feelings. Part of me feels like I am done with the whole "college scene" — the theme parties, the kegs . . . not as intriguing as they once were. In these instances, I am ready to make the transition into the "real world." However, it is scary to think that the days of sleeping late, meal plans, and Saturday football games are coming to an end. The best thing about graduating is feeling like the world is wide open with opportunity. I love the prospect of adventure and change.
>
> The worst thing is the unprecedented level of responsibility that comes with graduating. Suddenly, mooching off Mom and Dad for everything

becomes unacceptable and it's time to be proactive about employment and finances. This is scary!

Comments from another summer intern, Ellie, reflect some additional pressure beyond the responsibility:

I'm excited to enter the workforce. I only worry that I won't find a job that is satisfying and engaging that I will actually be able to enjoy.

And she adds, with no irony:

I hope to really enjoy my first job, while getting paid a lot. I am not really sure of what industry I want to go into but I am really interested in doing something that has a lot of interaction, both within the office and with clients outside of the office.

So she doesn't know what she wants to do but she wants to enjoy it and get paid a lot. Who doesn't? But **what is realistic for a first job?** Maybe it won't satisfy all the criteria. And maybe what she should be saying is simply, **"I just want to work so I can figure out what I am good at and what I enjoy."** To find her voice

I'm not trying to be a downer here or tell you that you should spend your life working at something you hate. Remember, a key proposition of this book is that you need to be finding your voice as well as your path. I heartily endorse looking for something you enjoy. But **you might not get everything in your first job.** I'll venture to say you probably won't. But whatever you end up doing, you need to be open to getting started. If you communicate that attitude, combined with a sense of what you do well, you will make a memorable and positive impression in any job interview you have.

I worry about putting too many criteria on your first job. It troubles me when I hear a lot of talk about what you expect in your first job when I interview you. Do you really think my top priority is helping you find something you enjoy? First and foremost, I need to understand whether you can help me get done what needs to be done. Do you have what it takes to be part of our team? Of course this is an entry-level slot, and I don't really expect you to know how to do everything. **I just want to know that you seem like the kind of person I could put in the spot and you would help us get the job done.** If you sound like you are too worried about enjoying the work, your career path, and how you will be moving forward, I worry that you will be **too focused on what comes next** and not on what we need right now.

Never forget that you are coming into an organization that is made up of lots of individuals, all worrying about moving forward and progressing in their careers. **We need to know that when we bring you in, we will all get ahead.** The team player analogies are used in our business because they accurately reflect the challenge of hiring. We need someone who can **work with the team and bring unique strengths.** Work is work, not school. Of course, you learn and sometimes have fun and there is often socializing but college it isn't. No auto-matic changes at the end of a semester. **A marathon, not a sprint.** And the more you tell me about working during your interview, the more impressed I will be, whether you were flipping burgers, balancing your family's budget, or volunteering at the animal shelter. **You need to convince me** that **I want to work with you,** not that you are the smartest or the best-read. I want the hardest worker, not the lucky person for whom everything comes easy.

The purpose of your first job

You may not want to think about this quite this way, but some candidates I speak to find it liberating:

The purpose of your first job is to get your next job.

There are two ways for you to look at this observation. The wrong way is to be overwhelmed by it. The wrong way is to think, "OH NO! I don't even have my first job and I need to think about my second job!" But alternatively it can help you relax about your search. I promise you, **the next job is usually MUCH easier to get than the first job.** Most people with some actual experience who reach out and say, "Well, I think it's time to move on," and who can bring real experience and perspective make much better interviewees than people just starting out. I tell you this because I think it may make it easier for you to interview for your first job. It means that **all you really want to do in your first job is start working at something related to what you think you want to do.** All you need to do is make me feel you are pretty much willing to do almost anything you are offered to begin.

You really can't make a mistake as a new graduate. **Whatever job you take, even if it doesn't seem to have much "path" potential, if it is in a related field, will certainly help you find your voice.** If you love it, great! How lucky are you? But if you hate it, I would say you are lucky as well. Knowing that you aren't looking for your "permanent" job, but rather your first job, should make you more open to taking a job and learning from it as you search for your voice.

Jessie told me that she had a wonderful internship at MTV Networks the summer after her junior year in college. She loved it, they liked her, and would hire her back when she graduated. She liked the company and the work and thought she wanted to stay in the media business. But she didn't know if she should reach out and lobby for a permanent job there because she wasn't sure she should take the job if it were offered to her. She was wondering if she would be closing herself off too early if she took it. **Maybe she should hold out for something else.** Maybe there was **some other perfect job out there** that would be better for her. She came to me for advice. What do you think I told her?

Take the job, Jessie!

You need to work. What is the worst thing that can happen? If you don't love it in the real world, **you can look for another job.** You stay in a job by choice. You don't have to stay. It's up to you to decide. So get to work and learn. While you are there look around, listen, and learn. Look for your path but don't forget to also listen for your voice. Pay attention to the way people are, to how they relate to each other, to what they say about their paths. It will help you to work; **take the job.**

Consider Joey. He was always artistic, a fabulous calligrapher. He loved advertising. I remember when he hung up Absolut bottles while other 12-year-old kids hung up basketball posters. **Smart, for sure.** Washington University in St. Louis. **Directed, not so much.** Sure about what he wanted, not at all. After one of our consultations, Joey told me:

> It was so great for me to be reminded that your first job does not have to be your dream job.
> I am very determined and often push myself very hard, so hearing that I have plenty of time to achieve the job that I eventually see myself in is comforting. As someone who ALWAYS has some sort of plan, schedule, to-do list, or agenda, it is so important for me to remember that finding work is an ongoing learning experience that cannot really be mapped out or predicted.

I've heard from several young people who offer some very valuable advice from their first jobs.

Alice, a graduate of Lafayette College, moved from her first job at Liz Claiborne to a job at Thomson Reuters working in investor relations. When asked about her first job, she said:

> Your first job will likely not be everything you ever wanted it to be. Still, **put forth your best effort, don't become complacent and be cognizant of other opportunities opening up around you.** My new position is much closer to what I had wanted to do originally. I saw the opportunity and I went after it.

Great advice, Alice. There are opportunities everywhere if you think of them all as a chance to try out different voices. Many young marketing professionals say it would have been easier if they had just been **more relaxed about the future** when they first started.

You know
you are ready
to move on
when
you have
considered
three things.

Beyond the on-ramp

I have learned that there are **three parts to work satisfaction** in this business. I offer them as a way to think about whether you may be ready to move beyond the on-ramp. I would argue that **these three criteria need to be met for you to feel that you are in the right job.** But the tricky part is that at any given moment in time they aren't all aligned. And, of course, how you weight the variables in the satisfaction equation changes as the rest of the circumstances of your life change. Nevertheless, I would suggest that you can know if you are ready to move on only once you have considered all three components. And it is always your choice. You are NOT a prisoner at work. You are simply **balancing the equation** (every day if you feel like it) and since there are many ways to balance it, the decision about whether and when to move on should be on your own timetable.

Satisfaction:

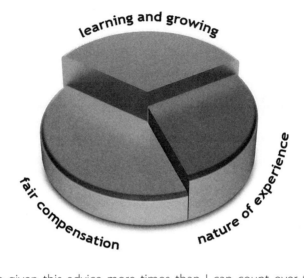

I've given this advice more times than I can count over the years I've been working, to more people than I can believe. I find that there are times when you want to balance the equation every day. The questions are:

1. **Are you learning and growing?**

2. **Are you being fairly compensated?**

3. **Are you having the kind of autonomy or experience you need at the moment in your career?**

Ask yourself the questions. If you **answer no** to all of them, then, of course, you are probably going to try to move on. However **even if you only can say yes** to one of them, you

may find that you want to stay put. These questions have always seemed natural to me and I've always thought they were **sensible criteria to use for evaluating a job,** but lots of marketing people I've spoken to struggle with them. I've had young people tell me they think they want to try going back to school but don't think they can afford it at a certain moment. OK? So you wait. I've had people say they want to go somewhere for more money but they're about to get married and it seems not to be a good idea to change everything at once. OK? So you wait. I've had people say they want to be transferred to an office overseas but they've got a sibling to watch out for in their current city. OK? So you wait. It's your choice, nobody else's, to stay where you are, if enough of the pillars are going well and if you can find satisfaction that way. Nobody can tell you that you must move on.

Question #1. Are you learning and growing?

It seems like an obvious thing to want in a job and you should be able to tell easily whether you are or you aren't. But I've seen that people sometimes get confused about when they are learning and growing.

As you are a beginner, I can't imagine that you aren't learning and growing, but it may not be as evident to you. Let's say you are lucky enough to be working for a wonderful manager, a highly skilled individual who also happens to be a great mentor. Of course you can learn a lot from this person and you should take advantage of the situation. But it is probably less clear that you are learning if you are in a job reporting to someone who is not a highly skilled individual and who isn't a great mentor. In that case, you may be surprised to know that there are lots of ways to learn, especially if you remember that you have been searching for your voice as well as your path.

First, you should be learning about the subject matter you are working on—the category or brand experience can be building your knowledge base, as well as your resume. And of course **you should be learning how NOT to manage.** Everything you experience working for someone whose management style you hate should be helping you develop a management style your subordinates will NOT hate. **You are learning what to do as well as what not to do, what you like and what you don't like.** How can you say you aren't learning and growing?

Question #2. Are you being fairly compensated?

That one sounds easier. I suppose it is. The only thing you really need to consider then, is that **if you go somewhere to do work you hate or to work for someone you hate simply because it pays more money you will soon find that the money wears thin.** You spend a lot of waking hours at work and it does pay to find something you like, something that allows you to express your voice. Many people who leave simply for money find that, after the initial thrill, the drawbacks often outweigh the benefits.

Money can't buy you job satisfaction. Really.

Question #3. Are you having the kind of autonomy or experience you need at the moment in your career?

As for #3, some people forget about this. At any given moment, your life may be making demands on you outside of work that require your attention. You've spent a year in your first job and now you think you want to move but your lease is up and you can't really look for a job right now because your roommate isn't sure he wants to live with you next year. Or you want to plan a wedding. Or you want to go to graduate school at night. Or the economy has crashed, and there really aren't very many jobs out there. Or you found out you are expecting a baby. **It just isn't the right time for you to look. So what is so terrible if you just wait it out?** We have already established that as a beginner you can learn about your path from every job, even one you are starting to hate. So maybe because of what else is going on in your life, you can benefit from staying. What is your hurry? **You are in control, you are making a choice to stay and besides you are moving toward finding your voice,** whether you like or don't like your situation.

A very experienced colleague of mine who hires and manages beginners and nonbeginners offered this advice. He suggests you periodically take stock. Make two lists:

Column A	Column B
Five things I **love** about where I am working.	Five things I wish I **had** or I wish were **different** about where I am working.
1.	1.
2.	2.
3.	3.
4.	4.
5.	5.

My colleague encourages you to look at the balance between the two lists. When you aren't satisfied with what is in Column A, you begin the process again. **Make a new resume and think about your new talk track. Because you will surely rely on both columns when you interview.** You will need to explain what you like about where you are as well as what you are looking to change. And this time you will need to focus on your accomplishments. You will need to tell me something about yourself and your old job in a way that makes you sound collaborative and competent, makes you sound impressive but not egotistical, makes you sound like someone who will fit in my organization and bring new thinking. But worry not. Just remind yourself what it took to find the first on-ramp and you will find subsequent ones as well.

In a work/life balance eXploring project I was involved with recently for a client, many new mothers told me that they were comfortable staying put, as they had already proven themselves to their current employer and didn't want to start that process all over again with a new baby. They were happy to have reached a certain level of autonomy and weren't prepared to give it up. **Staying put is a choice, not a jail sentence.** It's fine to make a voice choice for a period of time, even if it means a slower progression toward your path.

But of course if you've asked yourself the questions and you feel it is time to go, then go. **Don't choose to stay and be unhappy. Don't choose a path that you hate unless it helps you define your voice,** and even then, only choose it for a short period of time. Do the analysis and listen to your voice. It will help you find your path.

Wendy graduated from a prestigious communications school at an Ivy League university. **She lived the stages of this book once she left school,** and when I spoke to her she had a lot to say about **getting started and then moving on:**

At the time I got hired, I was ecstatic just to have a job. And the agency that hired me was big on social media, which is one of my main interests. It was a small independent interactive agency, and I was a Business Development Associate. I really enjoyed the laid-back, young environment, and the agency focused on entertainment which was exciting. I made $30,000 when I was hired, and $40,000 when I left, a year and a half later. I learned a lot, but by the end I understood what it meant when someone called my agency an "advertising sweatshop"—that's how I knew it was time to leave.

Wendy had a rough time finding her first opportunity. Although she had great grades and lots of courtesy interviews, she really had to network her way into her first company. She surprised herself when she found her second job much more easily. She successfully transferred from a teeny advertising shop into a much larger, prestigious firm. **By the time she interviewed at the bigger agency, she had lots to sell about herself in interviews.** It was relatively easy for her to develop her talk track because she could really speak from an informed perspective about what she liked, and what she didn't like. **She had experience to sell.** She could cite projects she had done successfully. Fundamentally, she had **found her voice and thus was able to move along her path.** The lesson is that you can really find your way if you know what you are looking for.

The standard recruiting and hiring process can confuse talent with experience.

The Y&R Way

All advertising agencies say they're committed to hiring the **best talent** out there. But often the standard recruiting and hiring process confuses talent with experience. People who look best on paper when they are just starting out may have spent too much time looking good on paper and may not really possess the talent we need. **At Y&R we are committed to hiring better talent, so we have to be committed to better hiring practices.** We aren't publishing this book to be nice. We want better candidates to want to come to us so we can do better work for our clients than our competitors can. With that as our objective, **we try to be smarter about finding and reaching out to new candidates** to make them part of the Y&R family.

In recent years, the advertising industry in the United States has been criticized for its lack of diversity, for not being able to ensure that minority talent is adequately represented in its management ranks. But in today's world, **a diverse workplace isn't just about multicultural talent.** We need many different kinds of talent if we are to continue to **innovate**.

Media and advertising change every day and it takes creative thinkers to shape the future. At Y&R we take our commitment to diversity very seriously. One of our senior account leaders tells me he always asks candidates what they would do with a brick besides build a house. He says that **he likes to see if they can think on their feet, if they can respond to a curve ball, if they can recover.** He isn't trying to be ornery, he is trying to get beneath **people's rehearsed answers** to try to predict their potential. He doesn't want to know what kind of animal or what kind of car they would be. He is looking for **creative problem solvers** and this question has been effective for him.

For more than 30 years, **Dorothy Giannone** has been responsible for finding our entry-level talent at Y&R. She has an uncanny ability to identify people that can, as my dad used to say, "punch beyond their weight class." Some years ago, Dot forged a relationship with CCNY, New York's premier public university, and its marketing and advertising program. As a result, we have relationships that ensure that **high caliber diverse candidates come to us.**

I asked Dot to explain **how she talks to new people** in order **to see beyond their inexperience and get them to reveal their potential.** Think about her words when you interview. Everyone at Y&R had to connect with Dot when we were hired. I can't say other agencies are as skilled at picking out the best talent even though I know they try.

Here is what Dot had to say:

I'm a people person, and what I do is try to understand the person sitting in my office. Entry-level people sometimes don't think they have a lot to say so I ask a lot of questions. I guess I am looking for a diamond in the rough. I want to see passion. **I want an answer to why they want to be in our business** and I don't want to hear that they were born to it, their mother was in it and it's in their blood. I do ask, obviously, about advertising they like and you would be amazed how many young people haven't thought about any. It seems obvious to me but I guess not to everyone. I expect them to know about our company—do the research.

I also look for something about their **presence**. Our business is about marketing and the way we say things matters. I don't want to see cockiness or arrogant confidence.

I look for **unique passions** and I listen to how they tell stories. And I try to understand how they will work under pressure to help me uncover how they will fit. I tell them the job entails collaborating with groups and multitasking and get them to describe something they have done that involves those sorts of skills.

One question I ask is for them to tell me about the best and worst thing that has ever happened to them personally or while they were working. This gives me an indication of how **open** they are and how willing they are to be **honest**. It can be anything, that their house burned down or that they flunked a class. I am trying to understand if they can learn from mistakes, if they can take feedback and direction. And I want to see confidence, even as they describe their worst experiences. It is easier to get **honest answers** from a story about something that really happened than it is when you ask people to talk about their **strengths** and **weaknesses**. You are looking for the same things but concrete stories are a better way to ask. I don't ask people about what kind of flower or animal they would be. I want to know about **what kind of people they are.**

I interviewed a woman who told me she wanted to learn to speak Japanese when she was six because she thought the calligraphy was beautiful, but her parents made her study piano instead. And she laughed when she told me that she studied piano but finally, after years of practicing music, she convinced her family they should let her study Japanese too. It was **an honest story, her unique story, and spoke volumes** about her passion and persistence.

Some people are worried because they come out of school and don't have three internships on their resumes. I would rather know that someone had to dig ditches to pay for college. That shows me a backbone and really tells me a lot. A person who has had to work while studying is clearly industrious and won't object to hard work. Think about it, a great GPA but no internship because you're paying your way through school by working in a bookstore. It really says something. **The star in college doesn't always turn into the star at work,** so if you've already shown me both, that's a great combination. People sometimes ask me if they should bring things they have written or projects they have prepared. Sure, but only as a basis for a conversation. **Practice talking about the project.** Describe it as a group effort. Use it to illustrate your negotiating skills as well as your creativity. I want a whole person, one who can work with us, not a lone wolf who needs a lot of space.

And of course there are a few things NOT to say. I've loved ads since I was 2? Nobody has. I once had a candidate say, "I don't like to work in teams; I'm better when I work alone." That's a real red flag. And **you've got to ask questions.** Of me when you interview, and of your boss when you work, so never be afraid to do so. **Ask questions that show you have thought about what you are asking.** Not things like what am I looking for, or how did I get started. Only ask those if I open the door to it. I want you to talk and I want to understand what kind of thinker you are. When you leave, you should feel like I've gotten to know you. Like you've told me what you are all about.

And once you leave **I do appreciate a thank-you note.**

One with substance, based on our conversation and not a form letter. Hand written or email is fine, but it better not be a generic form letter. I once received an email that was addressed to a competitor colleague. Proofread, even when you cut and paste. I sent it back to the candidate and warned him about the evils of technology and the need to proofread.

It's tricky really. There are no rules and lots of missteps you can make. But you have a lot of control. Tell me about yourself without bragging, convince me to buy but don't be too salesy. I trust my instincts and so should you. Sometimes it just comes down to how you tell the story. If that isn't advertising, what is?

As you can see, Dot asks much **more about people than skills.** Much more about personality than leadership. When we hire for a company, we are looking to hire people we'd like on our team. Those who can think independently but who want to work with us and will be willing to compromise. One thing this business has taught me is that two pieces of data are more helpful than a single piece. Two people thinking about a problem will bring a more creative solution than one person alone. **Nobody is really smart enough or talented enough in our complicated business to do everything alone.** So when you are interviewing, try to **show me why I want to work with you** and I will be much more inclined to do so.

At Y&R we always want to meet new and different people

in every department even if we have no openings. We try to make interviewing part of our fabric because it helps us stay on top of what talent is looking for. We try to accommodate a candidate's request for an informational interview. We offer shadow opportunities with surprising frequency so young people can become more comfortable with how work gets done in an agency. We are rather like the sports scouts who spend time in the field even when it isn't recruiting season— **we just want to keep current about who is trying to get hired and what they care about.**

Because we are so committed to hiring the best talent we have a number of ongoing initiatives in place to support our goals.

1. Our approach to internships

We love our interns. **They help us do real work.** In winter and summer Y&R hosts a large number of students who work on real projects. Some interns are paid, some receive course credit, but we take pride in the fact that all are productive. **We use interns in every department.** It helps us really get the measure of the students we host, and the professionals who agree to supervise interns take their roles seriously. Agreeing to mentor an intern is a commitment but it is one we believe adds value to the work we do for clients.

Our summer internship program is difficult to get into. It requires applications and essays. The program has been **designed to help students get real-world experience** beyond what they could get as part of a workshop class in the university setting. Unlike some agency programs, we expose our interns to real client problems or pitches as team members. That way **we benefit from their contributions and they learn real-world skills.** We are also able to assess their talents "in the field," which gives us a better ability to make job offers to individuals who truly contribute.

2. Our ongoing alliances

We work very closely with CCNY and New York's Fashion Institute of Technology (FIT) to attract talented interns. These students are supervised at Y&R during the school year, and both programs require students to share what they've learned with their classes. This allows others beyond those who work at Y&R to benefit from the internship lessons.

As an active member of the Advertising Educational Foundation, Y&R sends many professionals out into the academic world to teach classes and meet with students. Additionally, we host professors at our office from all sorts of universities, which helps us help them make their curricula more practical. This type of alliance helps us in two ways. First, **it gives us a great way to keep an eye on emerging talent as well as on industry issues.** Presenting at schools gives us exposure to quality students. And second **when professors come to the agency, our employees benefit from exposure to the latest academic thinking** which can help us improve the quality of the work we do for clients.

In the last several years, thanks to Dot Giannone, we have hosted "Winterns" from Tufts University. One of the most selective liberal arts schools in the country, Tufts does not offer a marketing or advertising degree. What they have is a minor program supplemental to their high-quality liberal arts program in Communications & Media Studies. The students compete to be allowed to **spend one week shadowing some of our employees**. They also come prepared to present a point of view [POV] on something they care passionately about. The winternship allows the students to learn something about our business and gives us a peek at some of the country's bright folks who might not otherwise find their way to advertising.

3. How we find the right folks

One thing we always do is ask our candidates to meet many people at the agency from many different departments. If you are a beginner in Account Management, in addition to your potential boss we might have you meet our Strategist or Creative Director. As I have said, **our business is about collaboration and we want to hire people who can work with people who may not always speak the same language, either literally, as we are a global organization, or figuratively,** as not everyone you work with will have identical training or even use the same jargon, depending on their experience.

The advertising business is in flux. **Media has changed and continues to change, and the worst thing we can do is**

Hiring **PLU** is **NOT** a future-focused decision.

hire only for today. Whenever I ask one of our most experienced Creative Directors to meet with a Strategy candidate, we have a laugh about how our business requires "different horses for different courses." He says **our clients are all different types of people, so we at the agency need different types of talent.** Many hiring managers make what I call **the PLU mistake — People Like Us.** I guess it is natural. As a professional, you see the world your way and so it isn't surprising that you would gravitate toward people who seem "like you" when you look at candidates. But that is shortsighted thinking. Hiring is a future-focused decision. Of course you want someone who can do the job you have open, but you really want to try to ensure that **the person can grow with the job** both vertically (get promoted) and horizontally (innovate as business changes).

We ask the right questions—and they're not necessarily all about the job we're looking to fill. Chapter 4 tells the story of Anna and her job at Bloomingdale's. **The experience she gained selling clothes made her right for advertising** even if it might not have seemed so on the surface. If we had interviewed her and only asked about her ad experience, there would have been nothing to discover about her and we would have missed a chance to get someone who is industrious, motivated, and collaborative.

We ask direct and indirect questions. We listen well and sometimes ask applicants **all sorts of seemingly random questions to better learn who they are.** We ask them to talk about themselves, to describe something they have seen that has shaped them, anything to help us learn more. Our experience in consumer insights sometimes means that we have them role-play a little as part of our drive to find out what makes them interesting and different. Management consultants have been known to use techniques like this and I've been told they find it to be very effective.

We want to hire diverse talent. We are building an agency, a collection of people with different skills who can work together. We don't assume a candidate's point of difference is a business skill, and we hire people with and without experience. **Great talent, especially unique talent, can be hidden behind what may look like an average skill set, especially in a domain like advertising.** When we try to understand what differentiates candidates from one another, we're really looking for the **passions, hobbies, interests, and qualities** that make them great people who can become greatly skilled professionals. **We can always train someone on skills,** and we do. But **we can't create a true passion that doesn't already exist** within the young person. We can't create a love for a hobby that inspires creative thinking. We can't create a commitment to a cause that invokes a sense of partnership. We can teach people to write and present well but we try to hire individuals who can work together, each with particular talents and strengths, to build a better company and do better work for our clients.

Debbie Kamioner, Associate Director of Recruiting at Y&R, looks for very specific characteristics in the people she interviews for entry-level positions. She sees people looking for work in every department—creative, account, and strategy. She has some **very specific qualities she is looking for** and uses all her questions to identify them. Debbie describes the qualities as follows:

1. Work attitude

2. Work ethic

3. Native intelligence

She defines **work attitude** as being about what it will be like to work with you.

You need to try to demonstrate that **you are going to do whatever we ask you to do, with a smile.** There are several ways you can communicate that, in your overall demeanor and openness, as well as by finding a way to tell me a story about a time when you did something tedious with a smile. Debbie really wants to think that **beginners have a realistic sense about the job.** She told me the story of a woman who convinced her she had the right attitude about doing repetitive tasks because she had been on her college swim team and had practiced boring flip turns over and over again. The young woman understood that if she made a mistake in her turn during a race she wouldn't win. She convinced us she knew what hard work was about.

Work ethic means that when a client calls and asks for something at the end of the day, a beginner isn't going to say that she can't work on it because she has a basketball game.

It also, of course, means **showing up on time and taking your job seriously even if others around you aren't** doing so. Debbie points out that sometimes when you are hired as an Assistant Account Executive, you might be working with some Account Executives who are tired of doing the work you have been hired to do. They may feel that they've paid their dues and are waiting for reward or recognition. As the "new guy," **you've got to work hard to keep focused on your own path.** As the newest member of the team who has something to prove, you've got to get past their grumbling. **When you interview for your first job, you need to seem like you can be** the one with the greatest commitment. Someone who is not looking for the easy way out. Again, telling a story to demonstrate work ethic is great. Describe jobs you have had with pride and illustrate the characteristics they tested in you. **Seem like you would be both thrilled and grateful to work with us.**

Native intelligence is less about "book learning or grades" and more about instinct, although we do expect you to be able to write clearly, present a cogent argument, and do so with a little flair.

That is what marketing is about. In this case, be sure to watch for **typos,** don't cut and paste a cover note from another letter and forget to change the company name. Be **careful** and **detail oriented.** Also demonstrate curiosity about our business. Cite sources you have read, talk about what you have learned about our company. What **industry publications** have you consulted? We aren't hiring you for "what" you know but for what kind of value you can add to our firm. Our clients need to know that we hire accomplished young people who are passionate and committed to hard work. But also **that these people can contribute to their strategic issues and are intelligent enough to signal problems when they run across them.** It goes without saying you need a cogent "elevator" pitch about yourself. I want to see that you are realistic about what you are all about and that you have tried to learn about the job.

Debbie says she does ask about **"interests"** outside of work and agrees that if something is on your resume, it is fair game for questions. She had an interesting observation about **too much focus on fraternity and sorority activities.** She feels that these could suggest greater interest in social pursuits than in intellectual or more productive activities. Again, it isn't a hard and fast rule, but be careful when you talk about your college experience and its relationship to work. She loves seeing work experience. People who work their way through school are industrious and capable. And they appreciate the value of work. She says that the way you talk about these jobs is important, but that candidates who have "flipped hamburgers" are often more impressive than those with internships based on family connections.

Additionally, Debbie had some suggestions about the final moments of an interview when she usually asks candidates if they have any questions for her. Don't ask, "Do you promote from within?" **Don't make us feel that you have a timetable or fixed expectations about your next job.** We want to know that you are committed to work, to the firm and its growth. A question that makes you sound too self-focused can undo some hard work you did during an interview. To me this sounds like Debbie is advising less focus on the "path" and more on your "voice." **Show us that you can deliver beyond company expectations and you will find your way.**

We try to do right by our people

Listen to **Chris Cutone,** HR Director at Y&R NY, who joined Y&R because she believed in our vision for our talent:

> We understand that **once we hire great new talent we need to protect it.** And we know that it takes **training** and **support.**

Our talent practices are designed to:

1. **Provide opportunities** for learning and growing. This includes formal and informal training as well as conference attendance and exposure to industry events.

2. **Deliver the appropriate balance between supervision and autonomy** to give people the experience they want. We try to make sure they have opportunities to socialize with coworkers and that we rotate their assignments so they get new experiences. Additionally, we are careful to help them feel supported in their personal lives as well as in their careers.

3. **Compensate fairly and competitively** and, when we have lean times and can't do so, we work hard to explain ourselves so our employees have reasonable expectations. When #3 becomes challenging, as it can when we face a business slowdown, a focus on #1 and #2 can go a long way to helping us retain our talent.

This book was written for young people trying to find the on-ramp to advertising. Written for them and to them. But it can be of value for people with a few years in the business who are growing beyond their first jobs.

We also believe this book can serve as **a reminder for anyone involved in talent management in our industry.** For all the managers out there, please note that I believe the next generation of talent will be even more committed to finding their path AND their voice. And so for the future of our business, we must be committed to helping them do both.

Afterword

If you are just starting out, **this book was designed to help you as you transition from school to work in advertising** by suggesting that you try to find your voice while you are looking for your path. It is my hope that in every chapter you can find something you can use. Some chapters may be more helpful than others, but all of them try to tell you stories that you can relate to in order to help you think about your voice and your path.

When I started at Y&R, like many of you I thought I was looking for a path. And when I got my first job, I found that it didn't really fit with who I was. In fact, I didn't love it and I didn't see myself as having much in common with any of the folks I worked with. I did business development support work and was anxious all the time while I did it. It wasn't good for my voice. But I was on a path and met lots of senior executives who would help me move along not simply to be nice but because it was good business for them. **They had learned to like and trust me and so wanted to help me.** At that time I thought the only way to go was down the same path as everyone else.

Do the business development job, then the assistant account executive job, then the account executive job, and so on. **It never really occurred to me that I could look for another type of path,** one that was more in keeping with my voice, because it never occurred to me that one sign of not having found my voice was that I was not happy on my path.

I got lots of advice that I ignored. My husband and my parents encouraged me to seek out work that made me feel good. When it was time to rotate jobs, my boss, a brilliant man who became the chairman of our company, told me he thought I should go into the research department, and instead of thanking him, I thought I knew better and argued that I had earned a shot at the more prestigious account management department. **I can't believe I didn't listen to him.** When I asked him whether he was worried that I couldn't be successful in account management, he said, "Of course, Belle, you can do anything. I just think you will like research better." It now makes me laugh that I didn't listen to him. Maybe I wasn't confident enough to choose a path that was different from the one others I knew had taken.

In fact, it wasn't until I went on my first maternity leave and had stepped off the path for a few months, that I saw clearly that I wasn't moving in a direction consistent with my voice. When it came time to go back to work, I realized that if I were going to leave my new son while I worked, **I would be miserable if I didn't think my job was matched to my skills, to my interests, to my voice.**

Years later when I think back on it, I am impressed by how right my boss was. I love research! After my second maternity leave, I happily enrolled in graduate classes at night in a research PhD program that would help improve my voice. Learning and growing remains important to me even today. **Finding your voice doesn't mean reaching a wall.** On the contrary, it means **understanding what turns you on.** And when you find it, you can be more successful. No matter what path you choose.

I hope this book will spare you some self-doubt. If you love what you are doing, maybe you have found your voice and that is great and I know you will find your path. But if you hate what you are doing, don't despair because I know that, too, will help you find your voice. **There is no right path; there is only your path.** And it is your voice that will take you there.

Acknowledgments

At the risk of sounding like an Oscar winner, I need to thank some folks. First of all the young people in my family; Will, Rebecca, and Willow, their friends, and all my friend's children, who came to me for help getting their first jobs and whose questions helped me understand the big gap between college and career.

Thanks to the Y&R employees and interns, past and present, from whom I learned what it takes to be a mentor. There would be no book if Dot Giannone and Adrienne Martin had not asked me to help with the Y&R interns.

I am grateful to the folks at Tufts CMS and CCNY. I owe a lot to the strategic planning team at Y&R, but especially to early supporters Will Johnson, Lindsay Tatelman and Christianna Gorin. Then there is the team that made this a reality—each more enthusiastic than the next—the folks at Paramount, Marc Rappin, Carter Murray, Kristina McCauley, and the irrepressible Caleb Lubarsky.

My parents always told me to write a book but thanks to the support of my heartthrob and best friend, Jim Frank, I began to believe people would be interested in reading it.

About the Author

Belle Frank oversees the development of communications strategies for key Y&R global clients including, among others, Pfizer and Merck. She co-leads a department of 15 brand strategists and is one of the developers of Y&R's BrandAsset® Valuator brand equity model. Belle is a member of the Board of Directors of the Advertising Research Foundation and has co-authored several pieces published in *Admap* magazine. She received an Advertising Women of New York, Trailblazing Working Mother of the Year award in 2007.

Belle teaches in the City College of New York Branding and Integrated Communications program and is on the Board of Directors of the Tufts University Communications & Media Studies program. She has a BA in French from Tufts and holds a master's from the Harvard University Graduate School of Education, where she studied human development and the effects of communication. She has also taken courses toward a doctorate in Measurement & Evaluation at Columbia Teachers College.

Belle is married to Jim Frank, a writer and golf-expert blogger. Her son Will is an intellectual property lawyer in New York. Her daughter Rebecca is a digital and social media analyst in Washington, D.C. They have very exciting dinner conversations about the future.